I0712051

365

Feminist Quotes

DAILY TRUTH FROM CLASSIC AND MODERN FEMINISTS ON THE MOVEMENT TO END MISOGYNY, SEXIST EXPLOITATION, OPPRESSION, AND THE PATRIARCHY

1

Why do people say, "grow some balls"? Balls are weak and sensitive. If you wanna be tough, grow a vagina. Those things can take a pounding.

SHENG WANG

2

Imperfection is beauty, madness is genius, and it's better to be absolutely ridiculous than absolutely boring.

MARILYN MONROE

3

You don't have to play dress up to be a feminist. You are a feminist exactly the way you are. You can be a woman who wants to look good and still stand up for the equality of women. There's no uniform for feminism; you are a feminist exactly the way you are.

MEGHAN MARKLE

4

What I've learned from myself is that I don't have to be anybody else. Myself is good enough.

LUPITA NYONG'O

5

It's important to teach our female youth that it's OK to say, 'Yes, I am good at this!" and you don't hold back, you only see the men doing it. And they're praised for it, and the women are looked down upon for it. But I feel like it's good to do because once you realize you're confident and good at it, then you're even better at what you do.

SIMONE BILES

6

So long as you write what you wish to write, that is all that matters; and whether it matters for ages or only for hours, nobody can say.

VIRGINIA WOOLF

7

If I want something I'll make it happen

KIM KARDASHIAN WEST

8

You deserve to be here. You deserve to exist. You deserve to take up space in this world of men.

MACKENZI LEE

9

I'm a firm believer in just having no shame in what you do and what you choose to do with your body.

CAMILA MENDES

10

It is easier to live through someone else than to complete yourself. The freedom to lead and plan your own life is frightening if you have never faced it before. It is frightening when a woman finally realizes that there is no answer to the question 'who am I' except the voice inside herself.

BETTY FRIEDAN

11

She is smart and independent and emotional. She can be confused. She can lose her confidence. She can have confidence. She is everything. She has a human heart.

GAL GADOT

12

Woman's degradation is in man's idea of his sexual rights. Our religion, laws, customs, are all founded on the belief that woman was made for man.

ELIZABETH CADY STANTON

13

Whether I am meant to or not, I challenge assumptions about women. I do make some people uncomfortable, which I'm well aware of, but that's just part of coming to grips with what I believe is still one of the most important pieces of unfinished business in human history—empowering women to be able to stand up for themselves.

HILLARY CLINTON

14

I'm not here to be perfect and I'm not here to be anything but my best, whatever that means for me.

JENNIFER LOPEZ

15

Women don't need to find their voice. They need to be empowered to use it, and people need to be urged to listen.

MEGHAN MARKLE

16

We do need women in civic life. We do need women to run for office, to be in political office. We need a feminist to be at the table when decisions are being made so that the right decisions will be made.

DOLORES HUERTA

17

I deserve better —such a dangerous, mad thought for a woman to entertain.

MEREDITH DURAN

18

To all the little girls, never doubt that you are valuable and powerful, and deserving of every chance and opportunity in the world to pursue and achieve your own dreams.

HILLARY CLINTON

19

Men have committed the greatest crime against women. Insidiously, violently, they have led them to hate women, to be their own enemies, to mobilize their immense strength against themselves, to be the executants of their virile needs.

HÉLÈNE CIXOUS

20

We're all supposed to be different. I want so badly to encourage everyone to say, "Who am I and how do I want to live my life?

ELLEN DEGENERES

21

Each suburban wife struggles with it alone. As she made the beds, shopped for groceries, matched slipcover material, ate peanut butter sandwiches with her children, chauffeured Cub Scouts and Brownies, lay beside her husband at night- she was afraid to ask even of herself the silent question-- "Is this all?"

BETTY FRIEDAN

22

I think that it's just important to feed yourself positivity. Feed yourself how beautiful you are. Feed yourself how you are special. Feed yourself that you are a light. Tell yourself that.

KELLY ROWLAND

23

A bossy woman is someone to search out and celebrate.

AMY POEHLER

24

But I feel that women need to have a voice. That's the basic right of the women, and that's global. When a woman says something, she shouldn't be judged or silenced because she's a woman. The first step to empowerment and feminism is freedom for a woman to be able to be who she wants to be without being judged or objectified. For centuries, women have always been told to be a certain way or behave a certain way, and it's time women decide what they want themselves individually.

PRIYANKA CHOPRA

25

Feminism just means that I love myself as a female and I also love men. I am a strong woman. Hear me roar!

KATY PERRY

26

Simply put, feminism is a movement to end sexism, sexist exploitation, and oppression."

BELL HOOKS

27

A revolutionary woman can't have no reactionary man.

ASSATA SHAKUR

28

I don't think that loving yourself is a choice. I think that it's a decision that has to be made for survival; it was in my case. Loving myself was the result of answering two things: Do you want to live? 'Cause this is who you're gonna be for the rest of your life. Or are you gonna just have a life of emptiness, self- hatred and self-loathing? And I chose to live, so I had to accept myself.

LIZZO

29

I'm not sure how we got to this place, where a girl's only value is in what kind of marriage she has, how capable she is of keeping a man happy.

AMY ENGEL

30

The only way for a woman, as for a man, to find herself, to know herself as a person, is by creative work of her own.

BETTY FRIEDAN

31

A slut is someone, usually a woman, who's stepped outside of the very narrow lane that good girls are supposed to stay within. Sluts are loud. We're messy. We don't behave. In fact, the original definition of "slut" meant "untidy woman." But since we live in a world that relies on women to be tidy in all ways, to be quiet and obedient and agreeable and available (but never aggressive), those of us who color outside of the lines get called sluts. And that word is meant to keep us in line.

JACLYN FRIEDMAN

32

There is no greater pillar of stability than a strong, free, and educated woman.

ANGELINA JOLIE

33

The heart of a woman will never be found in the arms of a man.

VANESSA CARLTON

34

I hate to hear you talk about all women as if they were fine ladies instead of rational creatures. None of us want to be in calm waters all our lives.

JANE AUSTEN

35

In reaction against the age-old slogan, "woman is the weaker vessel," or the still more offensive, "woman is a divine creature," we have, I think, allowed ourselves to drift into asserting that "a woman is as good as a man," without always pausing to think what exactly we mean by that. What, I feel, we ought to mean is something so obvious that it is apt to escape attention altogether, that a woman is just as much an ordinary human being as a man, with the same individual preferences, and with just as much right to the tastes and preferences of an individual. What is repugnant to every human being is to be reckoned always as a member of a class and not as an individual person.

DOROTHY L. SAYERS

36

Being a woman, in this world, ultimately makes you crazy.

HOLLY BOURNE

37

Man fucks woman, subject verb object.

CATHARINE A. MACKINNON

38

A feminist Is anyone who recognizes the equality and full humanity of women and men.

GLORIA STEINEM

39

Men are from Earth; women are from Earth. Deal with it.

GEORGE CARLIN

40

I myself cried when I got angry, then became unable to explain why I was angry in the first place. Later I would discover this was endemic among female human beings. Anger is supposed to be "unfeminine", so we suppress it - until it overflows. I could see that not speaking up made my mother feel worse. This was my first hint of the truism that depression is anger turned inward; thus, women are twice as likely to be depressed. My mother paid a high price for caring so much yet being able to do so little about it. In this way, she led me toward am activist place where she herself could never go.

GLORIA STEINEM

41

A lot of girls nowadays are like, "Eww, I'm not like that." They don't get that there's no one particular way you have to be in order to stand for all of the things feminism stands for.

KRISTEN STEWART

42

We need to reclaim the word 'feminism'. We need the word 'feminism' back real bad. When statistics come in saying that only 29% of American women would describe themselves as feminist - and only 42% of British women - I used to think, "What do you think feminism IS, ladies? What part of 'liberation for women' is not for you? Is it freedom to vote? The right not to be owned by the man you marry? The campaign for equal pay? 'Vogue' by Madonna? Jeans? Did all that good shit GET ON YOUR NERVES? Or were you just DRUNK AT THE TIME OF THE SURVEY?"

CAITLIN MORAN

43

If you want something said, ask a man; if you want something done, ask a woman.

MARGARET THATCHER

44

Barbie's disfigured. It's fine to play with her, just as long as you keep that in mind.

LENA DUNHAM

45

I am a strong and powerful woman. I am proud to be a woman and I celebrate the qualities that I have as a woman. I am not defined by other people's opinion of who I should be or what I should do as a woman. I determine that, not anyone else. I am not passed up for a position, title, or promotion because I am a woman. I fully deserve all the good things that comes my way. Irrespective of what anyone might think, being a woman places no boundaries or limits on my abilities. I can do anything I set my mind to. I celebrate my womanhood and I am beautiful both inside and out.

IDOWU KOYENIKAN

46

I think transwomen, and trans people in general, show everyone that you can define what it means to be a man or woman on your own terms. A lot of what feminism is about is moving outside of roles and moving outside of expectations of who and what you're supposed to be to live a more authentic life.

LAVERNE COX

47

I find it strange that practicing law in a comfortable well-heated office is considered too demanding an occupation for women, yet laboring from dawn's first light in crowded, drafty, ill-lit sweatshops is not.

SHIRLEY TALLMAN

48

Women's speech—and the fact that we are now listening to it—has enraged men in a way that makes them determined to re-establish the longstanding hierarchy of power in America. ... And yet this awful truth will not stop women from speaking, and I do not think that it will turn a movement into a moment. It has become clear that there is not nearly enough left to lose.

JIA TOLENTINO

49

There is a special place in hell for women who don't help other women.

MADELEINE ALBRIGHT

50

Good girls go to heaven and bad girls go everywhere.

HELEN GURLEY BROWN

51

For women, then, poetry is not a luxury. It is a vital necessity of our existence. It forms the quality of the light within which we predicate our hopes and dreams toward survival and change, first made into language, then into idea, then into more tangible action.

AUDRE LORDE

52

A culture fixated on female thinness is not an obsession about female beauty, but an obsession about female obedience. Dieting is the most potent political sedative in women's history; a quietly mad population is a tractable one.

NAOMI WOLF

53

I know what my mission is. I know what I'm hoping for and working hard for every day. And that's my focus. I'm not going to let people steal my joy. I move on. New day, new opportunity, new energy, let's go.

CIARA

54

They'll tell you you're too loud, that you need to wait your turn and ask the right people for permission. Do it anyway.

ALEXANDRIA OCASIO-CORTEZ

55

Women are always saying, "We can do anything that men can do." But men should be saying, "We can do anything that women can do."

GLORIA STEINEM

56

No woman can call herself free who does not control her own body.

MARGARET SANGER

57

A beautiful woman looking at her image in the mirror may very well believe the image is herself. An ugly woman knows it is not.

SIMONE WEIL

58

Society will not crumble if men take a turn at the dishes.

LINDA P. ROUSE

59

Do you think it is fair that guy will make more money doing the same job as you? Does it piss you off and scare you when you find out about your friends getting raped? Do you ever feel like shit about your body? Do you ever feel like something is wrong with you because you don't fit into this bizarre ideal of what girls are supposed to be like? Well, my friend, I hate to break it to you, but you're a hardcore feminist. I swear.

JESSICA VALENTI

60

When a woman is assaulted, one of the first questions people ask is, "Did you say no?" This question assumes that the answer was always "yes", and that it is her job to revoke the agreement. To defuse the bomb she was given. But why are they allowed to touch us until we physically fight them off? Why is the door open until we have to slam it shut?

CHANEL MILLER

61

I hate society's notion that there is something wrong with sex. Something wrong with a woman who loves sex.

ALESSANDRA TORRE

62

You don't have to be pretty. You don't owe prettiness to anyone. Not to your boyfriend/spouse/partner, not to your co-workers, especially not to random men on the street. You don't owe it to your mother, you don't owe it to your children, you don't owe it to civilization in general. Prettiness is not a rent you pay for occupying a space marked 'female.'

ERIN McKEAN

63

There is no gate, no lock, no bolt that you can set upon the freedom of my mind.

VIRGINIA WOOLF

64

To me, feminism is probably the most important movement that you could embrace, because it's just basically another word for equality.

TAYLOR SWIFT

65

I believe great people do things before they are ready.

AMY POEHLER

66

I always wanted to be a femme fatale. Even when I was a young girl, I never really wanted to be a girl. I wanted to be a woman.

DIANE VON FURSTENBERG

67

Usually when you see females in movies, they feel like they have these metallic structures around them, they are caged by male energy.

BJÖRK

68

Being born a woman is my awful tragedy. From the moment I was conceived I was doomed to sprout breasts and ovaries rather than penis and scrotum; to have my whole circle of action, thought and feeling rigidly circumscribed by my inescapable femininity. Yes, my consuming desire to mingle with road crews, sailors and soldiers, bar room regulars-- to be a part of a scene, anonymous, listening, recording--all is spoiled by the fact that I am a girl, a female always in danger of assault and battery. My consuming interest in men and their lives is often misconstrued as a desire to seduce them, or as an invitation to intimacy. Yet, God, I want to talk to everybody I can as deeply as I can. I want to be able to sleep in an open field, to travel west, to walk freely at night...

SYLVIA PLATH

69

You're sexist. I'm so sick of liberal lefty men practicing sexual discrimination under the guise of protecting women against sexual discrimination.

GILLIAN FLYNN

70

When you grow up as a girl, it is like there are faint chalk lines traced approximately three inches around your entire body at all times, drawn by society and often religion and family and particularly other women, who somehow feel invested in how you behave, as if your actions reflect directly on all womanhood.

M.E. THOMAS

71

Teach her that the idea of 'gender roles' is absolute nonsense. Do not ever tell her that she should or should not do something because she is a girl. 'Because you are a girl' is never reason for anything. Ever.

CHIMAMANDA NGOZI ADICHIE

72

It is never too late to check yourself and right your wrongs. I used to be slut shamey, judgmental, and my feminism wasn't intersectional enough. Nobody is born perfectly 'woke.' Listen, read, learn, grow, change, and make room for everyone. We aren't free until ALL of us are free.

JAMEELA JAMIL

73

My wish is to ride the tempest, tame the waves, kill the sharks. I will not resign myself to the usual lot of women who bow their heads and become concubines.

TRIEU THI CHOI

74

Women may be the one group that grows more radical with age.

GLORIA STEINEM

75

I don't know. I don't like girls whining and complaining about wanting a man! I never liked 'Sex and the City,' the kind of thing where women only feel empowered once they find The Man. It is just not up my alley. I don't believe in it. There is nothing you can control about love.

JENNIFER ANISTON

76

My mother told me to be a lady. And for her, that meant be your own person, be independent.

RUTH BADER GINSBURG

77

Don't allow people to dim your shine because they are blinded. Tell them to put on some sunglasses.

LADY GAGA

78

He is a gentleman, and I am a gentleman's daughter. So far we are equal.

JANE AUSTEN

79

A woman knows very well that, though a wit sends her his poems, praises her judgment, solicits her criticism, and drinks her tea, this by no means signifies that he respects her opinions, admires her understanding, or will refuse, though the rapier is denied him, to run through the body with his pen.

VIRGINIA WOOLF

80

I just say the truth about what I feel: I feel like women can do anything that they put their minds to. That's really the truth — I started off with just a dream.

NICKI MINAJ

81

A feminist is a person who believes in the power of women just as much as they believe in the power of anyone else. It's equality, it's fairness, and I think it's a great thing to be a part of.

ZENDAYA

82

The master's tools will never dismantle the master's house.

AUDRE LORDE

83

There's nothing a man can do, that I can't do better and in heels.

GINGER ROGERS

84

In almost every professional field, in business and in the arts and sciences, women are still treated as second-class citizens. It would be a great service to tell girls who plan to work in society to expect this subtle, uncomfortable discrimination--tell them not to be quiet, and hope it will go away, but fight it. A girl should not expect special privileges because of her sex, but neither should she "adjust" to prejudice and discrimination.

BETTY FRIEDAN

85

Women's freedom is the sign of social freedom.

ROSA LUXEMBURG

86

She is free in her wildness, she is a wanderess, a drop of free water. She knows nothing of borders and cares nothing for rules or customs. 'Time' for her isn't something to fight against. Her life flows clean, with passion, like fresh water.

ROMAN PAYNE

87

The most courageous act is still to think for yourself. Aloud.

COCO CHANEL

88

When a man gives his opinion, he's a man; when a woman gives her opinion, she's a bitch.

BETTE DAVIS

89

It takes years as a woman to unlearn what you have been taught to be sorry for. It takes years to find your voice.

AMY POEHLER

90

You can be naturally beautiful with acne or scars, cellulite, or curves. So, let's celebrate each other, and ourselves, as we are, as we will be, and as we were meant to be. Unique. Imperfect. Beautiful. And so incredibly powerful

LILI REINHART

91

I am a proud black feminist and womanist, and I'm extremely proud of the work that's being done. I'm a feminist who wants not only to hear the term intersectionality but actually feel it and see the evolution of what intersectional feminism can actually achieve. I want women's rights to be equally honored, and uplifted, and heard...but I want to see us fighting the fight for all women — women of color, our LGBTQ sisters, our Muslim sisters.

SOLANGE KNOWLES

92

Gender equality not only liberates women but also men from prescribed gender stereotypes.

EMMA WATSON

93

The thing women have yet to learn is nobody gives you power. You just take it.

ROSEANNE BARR

94

The rule seemed to be that a great woman must either die unwed ... or find a still greater man to marry her. ... The great man, on the other hand, could marry where he liked, not being restricted to great women; indeed, it was often found sweet and commendable in him to choose a woman of no sort of greatness at all.

DOROTHY L. SAYERS

95

The ultimate sexist put-down: the prick which lies down on the job. The ultimate weapon in the war between the sexes: the limp prick. The banner of the enemy's encampment: the prick at half-mast. The symbol of the apocalypse: the atomic warhead prick which self-destructs. That was the basic inequity which could never be righted: not that the male had a wonderful added attraction called a penis, but that the female had a wonderful all-weather cunt. Neither storm nor sleet nor dark of night could faze it. It was always there, always ready. Quite terrifying when you think about it. No wonder men hated women. No wonder they invented the myth of female inadequacy.

ERICA JONG

96

I hate men who are afraid of women's strength.

ANAÏS NIN

97

I can promise you that women working together - linked, informed and educated - can bring peace and prosperity to this forsaken planet.

ISABELLE ALLENDE

98

We need to reshape our own perception of how we view ourselves. We have to step up as women and take the lead.

BEYONCÉ

99

The idea that a woman can be as powerful as a man is something that our society can't deal with. But I am as powerful as a man, and it drives them crazy.

ALEXANDRIA OCASIO-CORTEZ

100

No country can ever truly flourish if it stifles the potential of its women and deprives itself of the contributions of half its citizens.

MICHELLE OBAMA

101

Feminism always gets associated with being a radical movement – good. It should be.

ELLEN PAGE

102

It's not my responsibility to be beautiful. I'm not alive for that purpose. My existence is not about how desirable you find me.

WARSAN SHIRE

103

Being single used to mean that nobody wanted you. Now it means you're pretty sexy and you're taking your time deciding how you want your life to be and who you want to spend it with.

CARRIE BRADSHAW

104

When there are no ceilings, the sky's the limit. So, let's keep going—let's keep going until every one of the 161 million women and girls across America has the opportunity she deserves to have.

HILLARY CLINTON

105

I earnestly wish to point out in what true dignity and human happiness consists. I wish to persuade women to endeavor to acquire strength, both of mind and body, and to convince them that the soft phrases, susceptibility of heart, delicacy of sentiment, and refinement of taste, are almost synonymous with epithets of weakness, and that those beings are only the objects of pity, and that kind of love which has been termed its sister, will soon become objects of contempt.

MARY WOLLSTONECRAFT

106

Let's let every single living human be what they want, and not assume that we all know what's best. Let's also fight for the rights and the freedom of every human, because we are all on the same side.

DOVE CAMERON

107

Men often ask me, 'Why are your female characters so paranoid?' It's not paranoia. It's recognition of their situation.

MARGARET ATWOOD

108

In the future, there will be no female leaders. There will just be leaders.

SHERYL SANDBERG

109

The emerging woman will be strong-minded, strong-hearted, strong-souled, and strong- bodied. Strength and beauty must go together.

LOUISA MAY ALCOTT

110

A job is a powerful thing. By giving a woman a chance to discover what she's good at and use her time, talent, and skills to contribute to her community, she not only can provide for herself and her family, but she also gains confidence and dignity. She will feel like she can take on the world.

SHAY MITCHELL

111

A consequence of female self-love is that the woman grows convinced of social worth. Her love for her body will be unqualified, which is the basis of female identification. If a woman loves her own body, she doesn't grudge what other women do with theirs; if she loves femaleness, she champions its rights. It's true what they say about women:

Women are insatiable. We are greedy. Our appetites do need to be controlled if things are to stay in place. If the world were ours too, if we believed we could get away with it, we would ask for more love, more sex, more money, more commitment to children, more food, more care. These sexual, emotional, and physical demands would begin to extend to social demands: payment for care of the elderly, parental leave, childcare, etc. The force of female desire would be so great that society would truly have to reckon with what women want, in bed and in the world.

NAOMI WOLF

112

I feel like young girls are told that they have to be a princess and fragile. It's bullshit. I identify much more with being a warrior—a fighter.

EMMA WATSON

113

Because when there is true equality, resentment does not exist.

CHIMAMAMDA NGOZI ADICHIE

114

I think it's time to give people comfort. You have to eat. You have to stop thinking that a certain body shape is ideal, because it's not.

LANA CONDOR

115

I used to think that confidence came from what other people thought about me — but now I realize it comes from what I feel about myself.

DEMI LOVATO

116

I am not free while any woman is unfree, even when her shackles are very different from my own.

AUDRE LORDE

117

I don't know why people are so reluctant to say they're feminists. Maybe some women just don't care. But how could it be any more obvious that we still live in a patriarchal world when feminism is a bad word?"

ELLEN PAGE

118

Breasts are a scandal because they shatter the border between motherhood and sexuality.

IRIS MARION YOUNG

119

A girl's got to use what she's given and I'm not going to make a guy drool the way a Britney video does. So, I take it to extremes. I don't say I dress sexily on stage - what I do is so extreme. It's meant to make guys think: 'I don't know if this is sexy or just weird.

LADY GAGA

120

I was the first woman to burn my bra - it took the fire department four days to put it out.

DOLLY PARTON

121

If you consider a woman less pure after you've touched her, maybe you should take a look at your hands.

KAIJA SABBAH

122

As long as she thinks of a man, nobody objects to a woman thinking.

VIRGINIA WOOLF

123

Wherever you find a great man, you will find a great mother or a great wife standing behind him - or so they used to say. It would be interesting to know how many great women have had great fathers and husbands behind them.

DOROTHY L. SAYERS

124

My movement is my movement. When all the dust has settled on the groundbreaking-ness, I'm going to still be doing this. I'm not going to suddenly change. I'm going to still be telling my life story through music. And if that's body-positive to you, amen. If that's feminist to you, amen. If that's pro-black to you, amen. Because ma'am, I'm all of those things.

LIZZO

125

I want a zero-tolerance policy on all the patriarchal bullshit.

CAITLIN MORAN

126

Teach your daughters their battle cries are needed far more than their silence and hear them deafen the world with their fearlessness.

NIKITA GILL

127

What feminism means to me is just standing up for gender equality and trying to empower our youth. And showing women that you can embrace your sexuality and you deserve to have confidence and you don't need to conform to society's views on what women should be or how you should dress.

DEMI LOVATO

128

The point is not for women simply to take power out of men's hands, since that wouldn't change anything about the world. It's a question precisely of destroying that notion of power.

SIMONE DE BEAUVOIR

129

He - and if there is a God, I am convinced he is a he, because no woman could or would ever fuck things up this badly.

GEORGE CARLIN

130

I love having every right to be as outspoken as I am, as any man would be.

CHRISSY TEIGEN

131

Some leaders are born women.

GERALDINE FERRARO

132

Fill your life with women that empower you, that help you believe in your magic and aid them to believe in their own exceptional power and their incredible magic too. Women that believe in each other can survive anything. Women who believe in each other create armies that will win kingdoms and wars.

NIKITA GILL

133

Men are visually aroused by women's bodies and less sensitive to their arousal by women's personalities because they are trained early into that response, while women are less visually aroused and more emotionally aroused because that is their training. This asymmetry in sexual education maintains men's power in the myth: They look at women's bodies, evaluate, move on; their own bodies are not looked at, evaluated, and taken or passed over. But there is no "rock called gender" responsible for that; it can change so that real mutuality--an equal gaze, equal vulnerability, equal desire--brings heterosexual men and women together.

NAOMI WOLF

134

As a young songwriter, I would put a lot of pressure on myself. I'd write a line and then aggressively backspace because I was like, "This isn't a representation of you!" or "This is weird!" I would just censor myself so heavily. I felt like there wasn't room for me to write a bad song or write something that didn't necessarily fit with my vibe or whatever. I think if I were to go back I would be much easier on myself. Write all kinds of stuff, man. Don't be afraid to cast your net wide creatively, 'cause I think that's the only way you're gonna learn about yourself as a writer.

LORDE

135

I just believe in equality for people, so it's not such a big deal. I'd rather be remembered for that than being an asshole.

EMMA MACKEY

136

It is time that we all see gender as a spectrum instead of two sets of opposing ideals. We should stop defining each other by what we are not and start defining ourselves by who we are.

EMMA WATSON

137

Because I am a woman, I must make unusual efforts to succeed. If I fail, no one will say, "She doesn't have what it takes." They will say, "Women don't have what it takes."

CLARE BOOTHE LUCE

138

There will be no mass-based feminist movement as long as feminist ideas are understood only by a well- educated few.

BELL HOOKS

139

In the public eye, girls and women with strong perspectives are hated. If you're a girl with an opinion, people just hate you. There are still people who are afraid of successful women, and that's so lame.

BILLIE EILISH

140

Why is it mischievous, fun, and sexy if a guy has a string of lovers that he's cast aside, loved and left? Yet if a woman dates three or four people in an eight-year period, she is a serial dater, and it gives some 12-year-old the idea to call her a slut on the internet? It's not the same for boys; it just isn't, and that's a fact.

TAYLOR SWIFT

141

No one is more arrogant toward women, more aggressive or scornful, than the man who is anxious about his virility.

SIMONE DE BEAUVOIR

142

I love saying 'yes' and I love saying 'please.' Saying 'yes' doesn't mean I don't know how to say no and saying 'please' doesn't mean I am waiting for permission. 'Yes please' sounds powerful and concise. It's a response and a request. It is not about being a good girl; it is about being a real woman.

AMY POEHLER

143

Some women get erased a little at a time, some all at once. Some reappear. Every woman who appears wrestles with the forces that would have her disappear. She struggles with the forces that would tell her story for her, or write her out of the story, the genealogy, the rights of man, the rule of law. The ability to tell your own story, in words or images, is already a victory, already a revolt.

REBECCA SOLNIT

144

The Victorian woman became her ovaries, as today's woman has become her 'beauty'.

NAOMI WOLF

145

It is vain to expect virtue from women till they are in some degree independent of men.

MARY WOLLSTONECRAFT

146

I love to see a young girl go out and grab the world by the lapels. Life's a bitch. You've got to go out and kick ass.

MAYA ANGELOU

147

Vaginas beat penises every time. They're like kryptonite. Penises are defenseless against them.

EMMA CHASE

148

My silences had not protected me. Your silence will not protect you. But for every real word spoken, for every attempt I had ever made to speak those truths for which I am still seeking, I had made contact with other women while we examined the words to fit a world in which we all believed, bridging our differences.

AUDRE LORDE

149

I feel now that the time is come when even a woman or a child who can speak a word for freedom and humanity is bound to speak.

HARRIET BEECHER STOWE

150

Regardless of the staggering dimensions of the world about us, the density of our ignorance, the risks of catastrophes to come, and our individual weakness within the immense collectivity, the fact remains that we are absolutely free today if we choose to will our existence in its finiteness, a finiteness which is open on the infinite. And in fact, any man who has known real loves, real revolts, real desires, and real will knows quite well that he has no need of any outside guarantee to be sure of his goals; their certitude comes from his own drive.

SIMONE DE BEAUVOIR

151

I think the girl who is able to earn her own living and pay her own way should be as happy as anybody on earth. The sense of independence and security is very sweet.

SUSAN B. ANTHONY

152

We are sisters and women need to stop being compared to other women. Beauty is not how we look; it is how we act.

KHLOÉ KARDASHIAN

153

Feminism isn't about making women stronger. Women are already strong; it's about changing the way the world perceives that strength.

G.D. ANDERSON

154

You may think I'm small, but I have a universe inside my mind.

YOKO ONO

155

A woman is human. She is not better, wiser, stronger, more intelligent, more creative, or more responsible than a man. Likewise, she is never less. Equality is a given. A woman is human.

VERA NAZARIAN

156

I am tired of living in a world where women are mostly referred to as a man's past, present, or future, property, or possession. I...do not belong to anyone but myself and neither do you.

ARIANA GRANDE

157

If any female feels she need anything beyond herself to legitimate and validate her existence, she is already giving away her power to be self-defining, her agency.

BELL HOOKS

158

The future is limitless, we can be anything we want.

TIFFANY YOUNG

159

Men make the moral code, and they expect women to accept it. They have decided that it is entirely right and proper for men to fight for their liberties and their rights, but that it is not right and proper for women to fight for theirs.

EMMELINE PANKHURST

160

Men should think twice before making widowhood women's only path to power.

GLORIA STEINEM

161

You can't be hesitant about who you are.

VIOLA DAVIS

162

I think that men ought to treat women like something other than weaker men with breasts.

JIM BUTCHER

163

The history of men's opposition to women's emancipation is more interesting perhaps than the story of that emancipation itself.

VIRGINIA WOOLF

164

Another world is not only possible, she is on her way. On a quiet day, I can hear her breathing.

ARUNDHATI ROY

165

I would have girls regard themselves not as adjectives but as nouns.

ELIZABETH CADY STANTON

166

As women gain rights, families flourish, and so do societies. That connection is built on a simple truth: Whenever you include a group that's been excluded, you benefit everyone. And when you're working globally to include women and girls, who are half of every population, you're working to benefit all members of every community. Gender equity lifts everyone. Women's rights and society's health and wealth rise together.

MELINDA GATES

167

If you say, I'm for equal pay, that's a reform. But if you say. I'm a feminist, that's a transformation of society.

GLORIA STEINEM

168

Women must learn to play the game as men do.

ELEANOR ROOSEVELT

169

Our men think earning money and ordering around others is where power lies. They don't think power is in the hands of the woman who takes care of everyone all day long and gives birth to their children.

MALALA YOUSAFZAI

170

More and more women are realizing that only collective strength and action will allow us to be free to fight for the kind of society that meets basic human needs.

ROXANNE DUNBAR

171

Women have to work much harder to make it in this world. It really pisses me off that women don't get the same opportunities as men do, or money for that matter. Because let's face it, money gives men the power to run the show. It gives men the power to define our values and to define what's sexy and what's feminine, and that's bullshit. At the end of the day, it's not about equal rights, it's about how we think. We have to reshape our own perception of how we view ourselves.

BEYONCÉ

172

Feminism is the radical notion that women are people.

MARIE SHEAR

173

One is not born, but rather becomes, a woman.

SIMONE DE BEAUVOIR

174

Men are afraid that women will laugh at them. Women are afraid that men will kill them.

MARGARET ATWOOD

175

As I started to explore my gender identity, I didn't know how I could claim the title of feminist without subscribing to the gender binary. I thought I had to be a proud woman to be a feminist. Then I came to the realization that I can be proud of women without necessarily identifying as one. A lot of people are rejecting the binary—that's the future of feminism.

AMANDLA STENBERG

176

Confidence literally starts from yourself. You have to go look in the mirror at yourself. If you don't like what you see, you're going to give off that energy.

MEGAN THEE STALLION

177

Never did the world make a queen of a girl who hides in houses and dreams without traveling.

ROMAN PAYNE

178

One of the reasons so many women say, "I'm not a feminist but..." (and then put forward a feminist position), is that in addition to being stereotyped as man-hating Amazons, feminists have also been cast as anti-family and anti-motherhood.

SUSAN J. DOUGLAS

179

What becomes of a man who acquires a beautiful woman, with her "beauty" his sole target? He sabotages himself. He has gained no friend, no ally, no mutual trust: She knows quite well why she has been chosen. He has succeeded in buying something: the esteem of other men who find such an acquisition impressive.

NAOMI WOLF

180

Culture does not make people. People make culture. If it is true that the full humanity of women is not our culture, then we can and must make it our culture.

CHIMAMANDA NGOZI ADICHIE

181

We know that when a woman speaks truth to power, there will be attempts to put her down... I'm not going to go anywhere.

MAXINE WATERS

182

I do not think I ever opened a book in my life which had not something to say upon woman's inconstancy. Songs and proverbs, all talk of woman's fickleness. But perhaps you will say, these were all written by men. Perhaps I shall. Yes, yes, if you please, no reference to examples in books. Men have had every advantage of us in telling their own story. Education has been theirs in so much higher a degree; the pen has been in their hands. I will not allow books to prove anything.

JANE AUSTEN

183

I am not afraid. I was born to do this.

JOAN OF ARC

184

I would compromise on a lot of details, but I would never compromise on love. And that kept me very focused through everything... When you care about something, you have to fight for it.

REBECCA SUGAR

185

You have what it takes to be a victorious, fearless, independent woman.

TYRA BANKS

186

All of the oceans and galaxies did not conspire together to create me just to I could reproduce for you.

AMANDA LOVELACE

187

Sometimes people try to destroy you, precisely because they recognize your power—not because they don't see it, but because they see it and they don't want it to exist.

JANET MOCK

188

Music is a male-dominated field. Women are not always taken as seriously as we should be, so sometimes we have to put our foot down.

MISSY ELLIOT

189

I love a bold lip color. I don't care. I don't care! I truly don't dress for men at all. I dress for me and what I think is cool.

LUCY HALE

190

I'd like every man who doesn't call himself a feminist to explain to the women in his life why he doesn't believe in equality for women.

LOUISE BREALEY

191

It took me quite a long time to develop a voice, and now that I have it, I am not going to be silent.

MADELEINE ALBRIGHT

192

I'm over trying to find the 'adorable' way to state my opinion and still be likable! Fuck that. I don't think I've ever worked for a man in charge who spent time contemplating what angle he should use to have his voice heard. It's just heard.

JENNIFER LAWRENCE

193

What's the worst possible thing you can call a woman? Don't hold back, now. You're probably thinking of words like slut, whore, bitch, cunt (I told you not to hold back!), skank. Okay, now, what are the worst things you can call a guy? Fag, girl, bitch, pussy. I've even heard the term "mangina." Notice anything? The worst thing you can call a girl is a girl. The worst thing you can call a guy is a girl. Being a woman is the ultimate insult. Now tell me that's not royally fucked up.

JESSICA VALENTI

194

No man is good enough to govern any woman without her consent.

SUSAN B. ANTHONY

195

I am a woman with thoughts and questions and shit to say. I say if I'm beautiful. I say if I'm strong. You will not determine my story—I will.

AMY SCHUMER

196

If you want to succeed you must never stop learning, never stop trying and just keep being yourself. You are your own person. You make the choices in life that affect you.

RUBY ROSE

197

We teach girls to shrink themselves, to make themselves smaller. We say to girls, you can have ambition, but not too much. You should aim to be successful, but not too successful. Otherwise, you would threaten the man. Because I am female, I am expected to aspire to marriage. I am expected to make my life choices always keeping in mind that marriage is the most important. Now marriage can be a source of joy and love and mutual support but why do we teach girls to aspire to marriage and we don't teach boys the same? We raise girls to see each other as competitors not for jobs or accomplishments, which I think can be a good thing, but for the attention of men. We teach girls that they cannot be sexual beings in the way that boys are.

CHIMAMANDA NGOZI ADICHIE

198

It is in vain to say human beings ought to be satisfied with tranquility: they must have action; and they will make it if they cannot find it. Millions are condemned to a stiller doom than mine, and millions are in silent revolt against their lot. Nobody knows how many rebellions besides political rebellions ferment in the masses of life which people earth. Women are supposed to be very calm generally: but women feel just as men feel; they need exercise for their faculties, and a field for their efforts, as much as their brothers do; they suffer from too rigid a restraint, to absolute a stagnation, precisely as men would suffer; and it is narrow-minded in their more privileged fellow-creatures to say that they ought to confine themselves to making puddings and knitting stockings, to playing on the piano and embroidering bags. It is thoughtless to condemn them, or laugh at them, if they seek to do more or learn more than custom has pronounced necessary for their sex.

CHARLOTTE BRONTË

199

I raise up my voice—not so that I can shout, but so that those without a voice can be heard. ... We cannot all succeed when half of us are held back.

MALALA YOUSAFZAI

200

So, we are speaking up for those who don't have anyone listening to them, for those who can't talk about it just yet, and for those who will never speak again. We are grieving, we are furious, and we are using our words fiercely and desperately because that's the only thing standing between us and this happening again.

EMMA GONZALEZ

201

No matter what you look like or think you look like, you're special and loved and perfect just the way you are.

ARIEL WINTER

202

The beauty of being a feminist is that you get to be whatever you want. And that's the point.

SHONDA RHIMES

203

The girls who were unanimously considered beautiful often rested on their beauty alone. I felt I had to do things, to be intelligent, and develop a personality in order to be seen as attractive. By the time I realized maybe I wasn't plain and might even possibly be pretty, I had already trained myself to be a little more interesting and informed.

DIANE VON FURSTENBERG

204

I would rather be a bad feminist than no feminist at all.

ROXANE GAY

205

A man once asked me ... how I managed in my books to write such natural conversation between men when they were by themselves. Was I, by any chance, a member of a large, mixed family with a lot of male friends? I replied that, on the contrary, I was an only child and had practically never seen or spoken to any men of my own age till I was about twenty-five. "Well," said the man, "I shouldn't have expected a woman (meaning me) to have been able to make it so convincing." I replied that I had coped with this difficult problem by making my men talk, as far as possible, like ordinary human beings. This aspect of the matter seemed to surprise the other speaker; he said no more but took it away to chew it over. One of these days it may quite likely occur to him that women, as well as men, when left to themselves, talk very much like human beings also.

DOROTHY L. SAYERS

206

Anything a man can do, I can do.

CARDI B

207

I believe it's time that women truly owned their superpowers and used their beauty and strength to change the world around them.

JANELLE MONÁE

208

No woman gets an orgasm from shining the kitchen floor.

BETTY FRIEDAN

209

I embrace the label of bad feminist because I am human. I am messy. I'm not trying to be an example. I am not trying to be perfect. I am not trying to say I have all the answers. I am not trying to say I'm right. I am just trying—trying to support what I believe in, trying to do some good in this world, trying to make some noise with my writing while also being myself.

ROXANE GAY

210

Butterflies are like women - we may look pretty and delicate, but we can fly through a hurricane.

BETTY WHITE

211

My coach said I run like a girl. And I said if he ran a little faster he could too.

MIA HAMM

212

They cannot stand that a refugee, a black woman, an immigrant, a Muslim, shows up in Congress thinking she's equal to them. But I say to them, 'How else did you expect me to show up?'

ILHAN OMAR

213

A woman with a voice is, by definition, a strong woman.

MELINDA GATES

214

For too many centuries women have been being muses to artists. I wanted to be the muse, I wanted to be the wife of the artist, but I was really trying to avoid the final issue — that I had to do the job myself.

ANAÏS NIN

215

Whisky, gambling, and Ferraris are better than housework.

FRANÇOISE SAGAN

216

Power to me is having the ability to make a change in a positive way.

VICTORIA JUSTICE

217

We need a feminism that is not negligent of women of color, trans women, queer women. We need a feminism that protects ALL women. Globally.

HALSEY

218

Her wings are cut and then she is blamed for not knowing how to fly.

SIMONE DE BEAUVOIR

219

By propagating women's nature as non-violent they are discouraging women from becoming fighters in the struggle for their own liberation and that of society.

ANURADHA GHANDY

220

Think like a queen. A queen is not afraid to fail. Failure is another stepping-stone to greatness.

OPRAH WINFREY

221

For I conclude that the enemy is not lipstick, but guilt itself; we deserve lipstick, if we want it, AND free speech; we deserve to be sexual AND serious—or whatever we please. We are entitled to wear cowboy boots to our own revolution.

NAOMI WOLF

222

It's a crazy time in the world. Women are the fucking future. And we're going to take over the world. That's really what I think.

DUA LIPA

223

Whatever women do they must do twice as well as men to be thought half as good. Luckily, this is not difficult.

CHARLOTTE WHITTON

224

You could make a case that, along with the technological revolution, the most provocative upending destabilizing thrilling change in the course of human history is that we're finally in it. ... We're here now, women are in the world, and we will not be bullied.

MERYL STREEP

225

Many of my movies have strong female leads- brave, self-sufficient girls that don't think twice about fighting for what they believe with all their heart. They'll need a friend, or a supporter, but never a savior. Any woman is just as capable of being a hero as any man.

HAYAO MIYAZAKI

226

There's nothing wrong with showing sexuality. If you have that inside, it's just an expression of who you are. If you want to share that with people, that's amazing.

CAMILA CABELLO

227

Equality is not a concept. It's not something we should be striving for. It's a necessity. Equality is like gravity. We need it to stand on this earth as men and women, and the misogyny that is in every culture is not a true part of the human condition. It is life out of balance, and that imbalance is sucking something out of the soul of every man and woman who's confronted with it. We need equality. Kinda now.

JOSS WHEDON

228

Sometimes, I want some damn makeup, and I'm going to wear it! Guess what — if I want to wear red lipstick and put eyelashes on, I can do whatever I fucking want. I am the creator of my own destiny.

ALICIA KEYS

229

If particular care and attention is not paid to the ladies, we are determined to foment a rebellion, and will not hold ourselves bound by any laws in which we have no voice or representation.

ABIGAIL ADAMS

230

One life is all we have, and we live it as we believe in living it. But to sacrifice what you are and to live without belief, that is a fate more terrible than dying.

JOAN OF ARC

231

The process begins with the individual woman's acceptance that American women, without exception, are socialized to be racist, classist and sexist, in varying degrees, and that labeling ourselves feminists does not change the fact that we must consciously work to rid ourselves of the legacy of negative socialization.

BELL HOOKS

232

Many women, I think, resist feminism because it is an agony to be fully conscious of the brutal misogyny which permeates culture, society, and all personal relationships.

ANDREA DWORKIN

233

Blessed be she who is both furious and magnificent.

TAYLOR RHODES

234

You don't owe prettiness to anyone. Not to your boyfriend/spouse/partner, not to your co-workers, especially not to random men on the street. You don't owe it to your mother, you don't owe it to your children, you don't owe it to civilization in general. Prettiness is not a rent you pay for occupying a space marked 'female'.

ERIN MCKEAN

235

What is feminism? Simply the belief that women should be as free as men, however nuts, dim, deluded, badly dressed, fat, receding, lazy and smug they might be. Are you a feminist? Hahaha. Of course you are.

CAITLIN MORAN

236

I think it's just as important what you say no to as what you say yes to.

SANDRA OH

237

Female friendships that work are relationships in which women help each other belong to themselves.

LOUISE BERNIKOW

238

You educate a man; you educate a man. You educate a woman; you educate a generation.

BRIGHAM YOUNG

239

Women belong in all places where decisions are being made. ... It shouldn't be that women are the exception.

RUTH BADER GINSBURG

240

I'm tough, I'm ambitious, and I know exactly what I want. If that makes me a bitch, okay.

MADONNA

241

She didn't care that people called her a bitch. 'It's just another word for feminist,' she told me with pride.

GAYLE FORMAN

242

A woman without a man is like a fish without a bicycle.

IRINA DUNN

243

No one can make you feel inferior without your consent.

ELEANOR ROOSEVELT

244

When God made man she was practicing.

RITA MAE BROWN

245

Sometimes I think the only real division into two is between people who divide everything into two and those who don't.

GLORIA STEINEM

246

Male domination is so rooted in our collective unconscious that we no longer even see it.

PIERRE BOURDIEU

247

The more I have spoken about feminism the more I have realized that fighting for women's rights has too often become synonymous with man-hating. If there is one thing I know for certain, it is that this has to stop.

EMMA WATSON

248

We walked through the streets with our protectors. We wore our dresses. We gave up our education because that was the price of safety. That was the bargain we made with the devil we knew to escape the devil we didn't.

C. J. REDWINE

249

If you don't see a clear path for what you want, sometimes you have to make it yourself.

MINDY KALING

250

I am a woman and a warrior. If you think I can't be both, you've been lied to.

JENNIFER ZEYNAB JOUKHADAR

251

There's something so special about a woman who dominates in a man's world. It takes a certain grace, strength, intelligence, fearlessness, and the nerve to never take no for an answer.

RIHANNA

252

One thing I'm more thankful for than just about anything is all that my experiences - including my mistakes - have shaped me and made me someone I'm happier to be — in songs and in life.

HAYLEY WILLIAMS

253

Cosmetic surgery processes the bodies of woman- made women, who make up the vast majority of its patient pool, into man-made women.

NAOMI WOLF

254

Being a feminist simply means you believe in equal rights, and I think if you ask anybody if they believe in equal rights, they'll say yes, man or woman. And if they don't—who the heck would say that?

LEIGHTON MEESTER

255

Other women who are killing it should motivate you, thrill you, challenge you, and inspire you.

TAYLOR SWIFT

256

Women will be hidden no more. We will not remain hidden figures. We have names.... It was woman that gave you Dr. Martin Luther King, Jr. It was woman that gave you Malcolm X. And according to the Bible, it was a woman that gave you Jesus. Don't you ever forget it.

JANELLE MONÁE

257

Maybe it just boils down to: I'm a woman who's really into her career, so I'm obsessed with the craft of my work. ... There's a romance in that for me.

MITSKI

258

I didn't know I had it in me. There's more to all of us than we realize. Life is so much bigger, grander, higher, and wider than we allow ourselves to think. We're capable of so much more than we allow ourselves to believe.

QUEEN LATIFAH

259

Women have to harness their power—it's absolutely true. It's just learning not to take the first no. And if you can't go straight ahead, you go around the corner.

CHER

260

Feminism is the radical notion that women are human beings.

CHERIS KRAMARA

261

Your sex appeal or beauty isn't defined by anyone else ... you are your own audience, your own V.I.P.

AMBER ROSE

262

It is time to effect a revolution in female manners - time to restore to them their lost dignity - and make them, as a part of the human species, labor by reforming themselves to reform the world. It is time to separate unchangeable morals from local manners.

MARY WOLLSTONECRAFT

263

Men's greatest weakness is their facade of strength, and women's greatest strength is their facade of weakness.

WARREN FARRELL

264

Women, if the soul of the nation is to be saved, I believe you must become its soul.

CORETTA SCOTT KING

265

I hate to hear you talking so like a fine gentleman, and as if women were all fine ladies, instead of rational creatures. We none of us expect to be in smooth water all our days.

JANE AUSTEN

266

Dear women, sometimes you'll just be too much woman. Too smart, too beautiful, too strong. Too much of something. That makes a man feel like less of a man, which will start making you feel like you have to be less of a woman. The biggest mistake you can make is removing jewels from your crown to make it easier for a man to carry. When this happens, I need you to understand, you do not need a smaller crown... You need a man with bigger hands.

HALLE BERRY

267

Feminism is layered and its power comes from its diversity.

SCARLETT CURTIS

268

I feel like I'm one of the biggest feminists in the world because I tell women to not be scared of anything.

MILEY CYRUS

269

I consider myself to be a feminist, and I'd always wanted to show that just because a woman has made a choice, a free choice to say, 'Well, I'm going to raise my family and that's going to be my choice. I may go back to a career, I may have a career part time, but that's my choice.' Doesn't mean that that's all she can do.

J.K. ROWLING

270

The saddest thing for a girl to do is to dumb herself down for a guy.

EMMA WATSON

271

Black women have had to develop a larger vision of our society than perhaps any other group. They have had to understand white men, white women, and black men. And they have had to understand themselves. When black women win victories, it is a boost for virtually every segment of society.

ANGELA DAVIS

272

I am satisfied that if a book is a good one, it is so whatever the sex of the author may be. All novels are or should be written for both men and women to read, and I am at a loss to conceive how a man should permit himself to write anything that would be really disgraceful to a woman, or why a woman should be censured for writing anything that would be proper and becoming for a man.

ANNE BRONTË

273

You need to find the power within to make things happen for yourself. When you realize this, you are unstoppable.

CHRISTINA AGUILERA

274

Do you really believe ... that everything historians tell us about men - or about women - is actually true? You ought to consider the fact that these histories have been written by men, who never tell the truth except by accident.

MODERATA FONTE

275

Feminism is for everybody.

BELL HOOKS

276

Of all the nasty outcomes predicted for women's liberation ... none was more alarming than the suggestion that women would eventually become just like men.

BARBARA EHRENREICH

277

Don't be afraid to speak up for yourself. Keep fighting for your dreams!

GABBY DOUGLAS

278

I wanted to be a part of telling women there is no segregation. There is no need to ever not feel beautiful or glamorous. There should be nothing that gets in your way.

JAMEELA JAMIL

279

My own sex, I hope, will excuse me, if I treat them like rational creatures, instead of flattering their fascinating graces, and viewing them as if they were in a state of perpetual childhood, unable to stand alone.

MARY WOLLSTONECRAFT

280

Feminism is not a dirty word. It does not mean you hate men; it does not mean you hate girls that have nice legs and a tan, and it does not mean you are a 'bitch' or 'dyke'; it means you believe in equality.

KATE NASH

281

But, of course, you might be asking yourself, 'Am I a feminist? I might not be. I don't know! I still don't know what it is! I'm too knackered and confused to work it out. That curtain pole really still isn't up! I don't have time to work out if I am a women's libber! There seems to be a lot to it.

WHAT DOES IT MEAN?

I understand.

So here is the quick way of working out if you're a feminist:

Put your hand in your pants.

a) Do you have a vagina? and

b) Do you want to be in charge of it?

If you said 'yes' to both, then congratulations! You're a feminist.

CAITLIN MORAN

282

Women have served all these centuries as looking glasses possessing the magic and delicious power of reflecting the figure of man at twice its natural size.

VIRGINIA WOOLF

283

Being female in this world means having been robbed of the potential for human choice by men who love to hate us. One does not make choices in freedom. Instead, one conforms in body type and behavior and values to become an object of male sexual desire, which requires an abandonment of a wide-ranging capacity for choice... Men too make choices. When will they choose not to despise us?

ANDREA DWORKIN

284

Women are brainwashed into feeling like we have to be skinny or sexy or desirable or perfect. One of the many things I was tired of was the constant judgment of women.

ALICIA KEYS

285

It's difficult to see the glass ceiling because it's made of glass. Virtually invisible. What we need is for more birds to fly above it and shit all over it, so we can see it properly.

CAITLIN MORAN

286

The success of every woman should be the inspiration to another. We should raise each other up. Make sure you're very courageous: be strong, be extremely kind, and above all be humble."

SERENA WILLIAMS

287

We teach girls shame. Close your legs; cover yourself. We make them feel as though being born female, they're already guilty of something. And so, girls grow up to be women who silence themselves. They grow up to be women who cannot say what they truly think. And they grow up--and this is the worst thing we do to girls--they grow up to be women who have turned pretense into an art form.

CHIMAMAMDA NGOZI ADICHIE

288

Feminism has never been about getting a job for one woman. It's about making life more fair for women everywhere. It's not about a piece of the existing pie; there are too many of us for that. It's about baking a new pie.

GLORIA STEINEM

289

And I knew in my bones that Emily Dickinson wouldn't have written even one poem if she'd had two howling babies, a husband bent on jamming another one into her, a house to run, a garden to tend, three cows to milk, twenty chickens to feed, and four hired hands to cook for. I knew then why they didn't marry. Emily and Jane and Louisa. I knew and it scared me. I also knew what being lonely was and I didn't want to be lonely my whole life. I didn't want to give up on my words. I didn't want to choose one over the other. Mark Twain didn't have to. Charles Dickens didn't.

JENNIFER DONNELLY

290

I am too intelligent, too demanding, and too resourceful for anyone to be able to take charge of me entirely. No one knows me or loves me completely. I have only myself.

SIMONE DE BEAUVOIR

291

You can't be afraid of what people are going to say, because you're never going to make everyone happy.

SELENA GOMEZ

292

There is no limit to what we, as women, can accomplish.

MICHELLE OBAMA

293

I love being single. It's almost like being rich.

SUE GRAFTON

294

Freeing yourself was one thing, claiming ownership of that freed self was another.

TONI MORRISON

295

Each time a woman stands up for herself, without knowing it possibly, without claiming it, she stands up for all women.

MAYA ANGELOU

296

Responsibility to yourself means refusing to let others do your thinking, talking, and naming for you; it means learning to respect and use your own brains and instincts; hence, grappling with hard work.

ADRIENNE RICH

297

Feminism is not about us convincing you that gender equality is worth engaging in only because there might be something in it for you, or in it for your sister or your mother. The question is, what's in it for humans? Happier, healthier, more successful children? Being able to take proper paternity leave and see your baby? Being able to talk to someone if you're feeling shit? Actually getting to be yourself? Getting asked out by a woman? Better sex? A marriage that is a true partnership? More diverse and interesting perspectives in art, culture, business, and politics? Getting to crowdsource all the innovation and genius in the world, not just half of it? A highly increased number of safe, confident, and fulfilled people on the planet, particularly women? World peace? Seriously. World peace!

EMMA WATSON

298

I love this neo-feminist idea—defining yourself as whoever, whatever you want to be today, and it can change tomorrow, and it can change the day after that.

UZO ADUBA

299

I don't feel like I need to be perfect. In fact, I think it means I need to let people know that I'm not perfect and that's okay. I try to just be an example of another person that's out there trying to figure it out, so that other women figuring it out don't feel like they're the only ones. It's a process for everybody.

ZOË KRAVITZ

300

There are techniques to learn about being one of very few women in the room, but that's why we have to elect more women, so we don't have rooms with only one woman — we have rooms with lots and lots of women making decisions!

HILLARY CLINTON

301

There is no female mind. The brain is not an organ of sex. As well speak of a female liver.

CHARLOTTE PERKINS GILMAN

302

In my music career, I've worked with two female engineers and one female producer in contrast to the hundreds of male engineers and producers and I find that very concerning. And I would like to change that.

TINASHE

303

I don't know if I'm a feminist, but I just know that I am all for outspoken, powerful women.

MAC MILLER

304

Life is not a competition between men and woman. It is a collaboration.

DAVID ALEJANDRO FEARNHEAD

305

When a door closes, you have two choices: give up or keep going. Let them shut you down or prove them wrong. We all start somewhere; it's where you end up that counts.

RIHANNA

306

There was a time when you were not a slave, remember that. You walked alone, full of laughter, you bathed bare-bellied. You say you have lost all recollection of it, remember... You say there are no words to describe this time, you say it does not exist. But remember. Make an effort to remember. Or, failing that, invent.

MONIQUE WITTIG

307

I get angry when women disavow feminism and shun the feminist label but say they support all the advances born of feminism because I see a disconnect that does not need to be there.

ROXANE GAY

308

There is no such thing as a woman who doesn't work. There is only a woman who isn't paid for her work.

CAROLINE CRIADO-PEREZ

309

I have sometimes thought that a woman's nature is like a great house full of rooms: there is the hall, through which everyone passes in going in and out; the drawing room, where one receives formal visits; the sitting-room, where the members of the family come and go as they list; but beyond that, far beyond, are other rooms, the handles of whose doors perhaps are never turned; no one knows the way to them, no one knows whither they lead; and in the innermost room, the holy of holies, the soul sits alone and waits for a footstep that never comes.

EDITH WHARTON

310

It's about pushing boundaries. I believe absolutely, the world wants something different, people want back their individuality.

PAT McGRATH

311

Taught from their infancy that beauty is woman's scepter, the mind shapes itself to the body, and roaming round its gilt cage, only seeks to adorn its prison.

MARY WOLLSTONECRAFT

312

I think the best role models for women are people who are fruitfully and confidently themselves, who bring light into the world.

MERYL STREEP

313

No woman can call herself free who does not own and control her body. No woman can call herself free until she can choose consciously whether she will or will not be a mother.

MARGARET SANGER

314

Comrades, there is no true social revolution without the liberation of women. May my eyes never see, and my feet never take me to a society where half the people are held in silence. I hear the roar of women's silence. I sense the rumble of their storm and feel the fury of their revolt.

THOMAS SANKARA

315

For too long, women have not been heard or believed if they dare speak the truth to the power of those men. But their time is up. Their time is up.

OPRAH WINFREY

316

I don't need a bedroom to prove my womanliness. I can convey just as much sex appeal picking apples off a tree or standing in the rain.

AUDREY HEPBURN

317

In my opinion, the most exciting potential of women of color formations resides in the possibility of politicizing this identity—basing the identity on politics rather than the politics on identity.

ANGELA DAVIS

318

When, however, one reads of a witch being ducked, of a woman possessed by devils, of a wise woman selling herbs, or even of a very remarkable man who had a mother, then I think we are on the track of a lost novelist, a suppressed poet, of some mute and inglorious Jane Austen, some Emily Bronte who dashed her brains out on the moor or mopped and mowed about the highways crazed with the torture that her gift had put her to. Indeed, I would venture to guess that Anon, who wrote so many poems without signing them, was often a woman.

VIRGINIA WOOLF

319

The enormous difference between fighting gender discrimination as opposed to race discrimination is good people immediately perceive race discrimination as evil and intolerable. But when I talked about sex-based discrimination, I got the response, 'What are you talking about? Women are treated ever so much better than men!

RUTH BADER GINSBURG

320

It is impossible for you to do it,' was the terrible verdict. 'In the first place you are a woman and would need a protector, and even if it were possible for you to travel alone you would need to carry so much baggage that it would detain you in making rapid changes. Besides you speak nothing but English, so there is no use talking about it; no one but a man can do this.' 'Very well,' I said angrily, 'Start the man, and I'll start the same day for some other newspaper and beat him.'

NELLIE BLY

321

I myself have never been able to find out precisely what feminism is: I only know that people call me a feminist whenever I express sentiments that differentiate me from a doormat, or a prostitute.

REBECCA WEST

322

Women are leaders everywhere you look—from the CEO who runs a Fortune 500 company to the housewife who raises her children and heads her household. Our country was built by strong women, and we will continue to break down walls and defy stereotypes.

NANCY PELOSI

323

Only stupid men would want stupid wives!

ROBERT THIER

324

Justice is about making sure that being polite is not the same thing as being quiet. In fact, often times, the most righteous thing you can do is shake the table.

ALEXANDRIA OCASIO-CORTEZ

325

We need women at all levels, including the top, to change the dynamic, reshape the conversation, to make sure women's voices are heard and heeded, not overlooked and ignored.

SHERYL SANDBERG

326

I cannot understand anti-abortion arguments that center on the sanctity of life. As a species we've fairly comprehensively demonstrated that we don't believe in the sanctity of life. The shrugging acceptance of war, famine, epidemic, pain, and life- long poverty shows us that, whatever we tell ourselves, we've made only the most feeble of efforts to really treat human life as sacred.

CAITLIN MORAN

327

A woman reading Playboy feels a little like a Jew reading a Nazi manual.

GLORIA STEINEM

328

I do not wish women to have power over men; but over themselves.

MARY SHELLEY

329

Of course, I am not worried about intimidating men. The type of man who will be intimidated by me is exactly the type of man I have no interest in.

CHIMAMANDA NGOZI ADICHIE

330

Am I bossy? Absolutely. I don't like to lose, and if I'm told 'no', then I find another way to get my 'yes.'

NAOMI CAMPBELL

331

It's my deep belief...that we should all feel deserved and supported in expressing our right being our whole selves, limited by nothing, regardless of ethnicity, gender identity, sexuality, ability, religion, or any other identity that we choose.

YARA SHAHIDI

332

Great minds may have cold hearts. Form but no color. It is an incompleteness. And so, they are afraid of any woman who both thinks and feels deeply.

SENA JETER NASLUND

333

No woman should be told she can't make decisions about her own body. When women's rights are under attack, we fight back.

KAMALA HARRIS

334

What I am proud of, what seems so simply clear, is that feminism is a way to fight for justice, always in short supply.

BARBARA STRICKLAND

335

The most important thing we can do is elevate the lived experiences and voices of actual trans people, so people aren't talking about us without us being at the table, without us being in the room. We have to empower trans people by lifting up their experiences and their stories.

LAVERNE COX

336

Sadly, the signals that allow men and women to find the partners who most please them are scrambled by the sexual insecurity initiated by beauty thinking. A woman who is self-conscious can't relax to let her sensuality come into play. If she is hungry she will be tense. If she is "done up" she will be on the alert for her reflection in his eyes. If she is ashamed of her body, its movement will be stilled. If she does not feel entitled to claim attention, she will not demand that airspace to shine in. If his field of vision has been boxed in by "beauty"--a box continually shrinking--he simply will not see her, his real love, standing right before him.

NAOMI WOLF

337

Human rights are women's rights, and women's rights are human rights. Let us not forget that among those rights are the right to speak freely--and the right to be heard.

HILLARY CLINTON

338

We should stop calling feminists 'feminists' and just start calling people who aren't feminist 'sexist'—and then everyone else is just a human. You are either a normal person or a sexist. People get a label when they're bad.

MAISIE WILLIAMS

339

You can tell whether some misogynistic societal pressure is being exerted on women by calmly enquiring, 'And are the men doing this, as well?' If they aren't, chances are you're dealing with what we strident feminists refer to as 'some total fucking bullshit'.

CAITLIN MORAN

340

Though we have the courage to raise our daughters more like our sons, we've rarely had the courage to raise our sons like our daughters.

GLORIA STEINEM

341

I did everything he did backwards and in high heels.

GINGER ROGERS

342

As a woman you are better off in life earning your own money. You couldn't prevent your husband from leaving you or taking another wife, but you could have some of your dignity if you didn't have to beg him for financial support.

AYAAN HIRSI ALI

343

Power is not given to you. You have to take it.

BEYONCÉ

344

My fucking voice is going to be heard.

MILEY CYRUS

345

If you obey all the rules, you miss all the fun.

KATHARINE HEPBURN

346

When men are oppressed, it's a tragedy. When women are oppressed, it's tradition.

LETTY COTTIN POGREBIN

347

Her mother told her she could grow up to be anything she wanted to be, so she grew up to become the strongest of the strong, the strangest of the strange, the wildest of the wild, the wolf leading wolves.

NIKITA GILL

348

My idea of feminism is self-determination, and it's very open-ended: every woman has the right to become herself and do whatever she needs to do.

ANI DiFRANCO

349

Well, knowledge is a fine thing, and Mother Eve thought so; but she smarted so severely for hers, that most of her daughters have been afraid of it since.

ABIGAIL ADAMS

350

Feminism is hated because women are hated. Antifeminism is a direct expression of misogyny; it is the political defense of woman hating.

ANDREA DWORKIN

351

We have to free half of the human race, the women, so that they can help to free the other half.

EMMELINE PANKHURST

352

Women, we endure those cuts in so many ways that we don't even notice we're cut. We are living with small, tiny cuts, and we are bleeding every single day. And we're still getting up.

MICHELLE OBAMA

353

Many people carry this type of negative self-image for years, but it is swept away the instant they experience their own perfectly clean space. This drastic change in self-perception, the belief that you can do anything if you set your mind to it, transforms behavior and lifestyles.

MARIE KONDO

354

Around the world there are countless examples of women rising, taking leadership, taking their destiny into their own hands, inspiring all of us. But women and girls are still the majority of the victims of war. They are over half of all refugees, and the vast majority of the victims of rape and other sexual and gender-based violence.

ANGELINA JOLIE

355

Then, people expect women to be that easy to understand, and women are mad at themselves for not being that simple- When in actuality, women ARE complicated. Women are multifaceted. Not because women are crazy. But because people are crazy, and women happen to be people.

TAVI GEVINSON

356

I hope that my presence on your screen and my face in magazines may lead you young girls on a beautiful journey, that you will feel validation of your external beauty, but also get to the deeper business of being beautiful inside.

LUPITA NYONG'O

357

Value yourself for what the media doesn't - your intelligence, your street smarts, your ability to play a kick-ass game of pool, whatever. So long as it's not just valuing yourself for your ability to look hot in a bikini and be available to men, it's an improvement.

JESSICA VALENTI

358

.."Fun?" you ask. "Weren't feminists these grim- faced, humorless, antifamily, karate-chopping ninjas who were bitter because they couldn't get a man?" Well, in fact the problem was that all too many of them HAD gotten a man, married him, had his kids, and then discovered that, as mothers, they were never supposed to have their own money, their own identity, their own aspirations, time to pee, or a brain. And yes, some women indeed became bad-tempered as a result. After all, no anger, no social change.

SUSAN J. DOUGLAS

359

Women have discovered that they cannot rely on men's chivalry to give them justice.

HELEN KELLER

360

It's hard not to be a fighter when you're constantly under siege.

CASSANDRA DUFFY

361

Never let anyone try and make you into something that you're not. Remember what it is that you want, and always stay strong in that.

ABIGAIL BRESLIN

362

That man over there says that women need to be helped into carriages, and lifted over ditches, and to have the best place everywhere. Nobody ever helps me into carriages, or over mud-puddles, or gives me any best place! And ain't I a woman?

SOJOURNER TRUTH

363

I think that any female who gets asked if she's a feminist... it's silly... it's so interesting when people ask females if they're a feminist. Of course, every female wants to be equal!

MELANIE MARTINEZ

364

Here's my feeling: For everyone, men and women, it's important to be a feminist. It's important to have female characters. It's wonderful for women to mentor other women, but it's just as important for women to mentor men and vice versa. In my line of work, having Greg Daniels be such a great mentor to me is fantastic. Finding a writer's assistant, be it a man or a woman, and encouraging them to think with a feminist perspective, is key.

MINDY KALING

365

My hope for the future, not just in the music industry, but in every young girl I meet, is that they all realize their worth and ask for it.

TAYLOR SWIFT